POURED OUT

ISBN 978-1-0877-4441-4
Item 005831829
Dewey Decimal Classification Number: 242
Subject Heading: DEVOTIONAL LITERATURE / BIBLE STUDY AND TEACHING / GOD

Printed in the United States of America

Student Ministry Publishing
Lifeway Resources
One Lifeway Plaza
Nashville, Tennessee 37234

We believe that the Bible has God for its author; salvation for its end; and truth, without any mixture of error, for its matter and that all Scripture is totally true and trustworthy. To review Lifeway's doctrinal guideline, please visit www.lifeway.com/doctrinalguideline.

Unless otherwise noted, all Scripture quotations are taken from the Christian Standard Bible®, Copyright © 2017 by Holman Bible Publishers. Used by permission. Christian Standard Bible® and CSB® are federally registered trademarks of Holman Bible Publishers. Scripture quotations marked (ESV) are from the ESV® Bible (The Holy Bible, English Standard Version®), copyright © 2001 by Crossway, a publishing ministry of Good News Publishers. Used by permission. All rights reserved.

publishing team

Director, Student Ministry
Ben Trueblood

Manager, Student Ministry Publishing
John Paul Basham

Editorial Team Leader
Karen Daniel

Writer
Angela Sanders

Content Editor
Stephanie Cross

Production Editor
Brooke Hill

Graphic Designer
Jon Rodda

TABLE OF CONTENTS

INTRO

For girls, some days it feels like there is no in-between, no safe space to exist as we were created: we are either soft or strong; well-behaved or history-makers; servant-hearted or ambitious; gentle or bold; poured out or fulfilled. But the truth of the matter is that God has called us to honor Him in walking the line between the extremes. When we look at the women throughout the Bible—and the God-fearing women throughout history—we see that their character and success were defined by God's call on their lives rather than the way the rest of the world saw them.

When we think of Elisabeth Elliot, we think of both the brave woman who faced the very people who murdered her husband and the compassionate missionary who longed to show them the beauty of forgiveness in Christ. In Rahab, we see the woman who hid spies at the risk of her own life because her heart had become softened toward God and His people— and the woman who became part of Jesus' own lineage. And in the Proverbs 31 woman, we see a business-savvy pillar of the home and community who also had a deep love for her family and was known for her godly character. They walked the line of living boldly for God, while gently calling others to "come and see" who Jesus really is (John 4:29).

Living poured out for God and learning to lead like Jesus doesn't mean your life is empty, but filled with Jesus. Being poured out means we do empty ourselves of our own desires to pursue God's, but He fills us with His Spirit who empowers us to go out and do His work. And being poured out also means that we, like Jesus, walk in gentleness and humility as we recognize that our purpose and our lives belong to God.

Over the next 30 days, dig deep into Scripture as we learn about what it truly means to live poured out—understanding what gentleness is and how Jesus' examples of gentleness lead us to live gently, too.

GETTING STARTED

This devotional contains 30 days of content, broken down into sections. Each day is divided into three elements—discover, delight, and display— to help you answer core questions related to Scripture.

discover

This section helps you examine the passage in light of who God is and determine what it says about your identity in relationship to Him. Included here is the daily Scripture reading, focus passage, along with illustrations and commentary to guide you as you explore God's Word.

delight

In this section, you'll be challenged by questions and activities that help you see how God is alive and active in every detail of His Word and your life.

display

Here's where you take action. Display calls you to apply what you've learned through each day's study.

Each day also includes a prayer activity at the conclusion of the devotion.

Throughout the devotional, you'll also find extra articles and activities to help you connect with the topic personally, such as Scripture memory verses, additional resources, and questions.

Poured Out

DAY 1

JESUS, OUR BURDEN LIFTER

discover

READ MATTHEW 11:28-30.

*"Come to me, all of you who are weary and burdened, and
I will give you rest. Take up my yoke and learn from me, because
I am lowly and humble in heart, and you will find rest for
your souls. For my yoke is easy and my burden is light."*

Everyone grows weary—or worn out and exhausted—sometimes.
Life is just as difficult as it is good, but those who don't yet know
Jesus experience a weariness that goes soul deep. They struggle
under the weight of sin, but they don't have to.

When Jesus died on the cross, He took the sin of the whole world
upon Himself and made forgiveness possible. When Jesus rose
again, He gave us the ability to have eternal life. All we have to
do to be set free from sin is put our faith in this gospel—or good
news—by surrendering control of our lives to Jesus. When we do,
the Holy Spirit makes us brand-new and comes to live inside of us.
God adopts us, and we become citizens of His eternal kingdom.

Life will always be difficult, but our souls don't have to remain
weary. Jesus promised to share our burdens, which are light in
comparison to the profound blessing of knowing Him. Even when
we struggle or fail, Jesus remains. Trustworthy and gentle, He does
not condemn, but leads by example, inspires with His love, and
empowers us to obey. All we have to do is let Him.

delight

What kind of weariness do you typically experience, and where do you think it comes from?

What must you do to experience the kind of rest Jesus offers?

display

In the days ahead, make an intentional effort to focus and rely on Jesus as you obey God. Follow His example and imitate His gentle spirit.

If you are weary from carrying the weight of your own sin, Jesus wants to lift your burden. Consider putting your faith in the good news of Jesus' death and resurrection by making Him Lord—or the boss—of your life. If you need help doing so, talk to someone in your church whose words and actions prove they know Jesus and ask them to show you how to express your desires and intentions to God.

Spend a few moments talking with God. Thank Him for sending Jesus to lift the burden of your sin. Ask Him to get your attention when your focus drifts and you forget to let Jesus help you keep living the way God wants you to.

Poured Out

DAY 2

SAVIOR BY CHOICE

READ 1 PETER 2:21-25.

He did not commit sin, and no deceit was found in His mouth; when
He was insulted, He did not insult in return; when he suffered, He
did not threaten but entrusted Himself to the One Who judges justly.
—1 Peter 2:22-23

When Jesus lived on earth, He was human like we are, but He was also God. He is a member of the Trinity, along with God the Father and the Holy Spirit. He shares deity and attributes with them, but differs from them in personality and function. Unlike the rest of us, Jesus played an important role in the creation of the world and has authority over everything we see and everything we don't see.

Nothing and no one has power over Jesus. Even so, Jesus allowed Himself to be crucified. What He suffered was undeserved because He never sinned, but Jesus was not a victim. Make no mistake, Jesus died on His own terms. Humans nailed Him to the cross, but He had the power to come down any time He wanted. Jesus was not overcome. He was simply committed to God's plan and purpose over His own rights and comfort, and we benefit from the gentleness He displayed.

All this being true, those of us who have surrendered control of our lives to Him must follow His example, laying aside our human rights as God asks us to in service to His plan and purpose. When we do, the world sees Jesus in us, and God is glorified.

delight

How has Jesus' gentleness affected your life?

What does the fact that Jesus laid down His life willingly do to the excuses we make when God asks us to sacrifice for others?

display

Consider how your life would be different if Jesus had decided not to obey God and lay down His life for your sin on the cross. Imagine how it would feel not to know Him or have the assurance of eternal life His sacrifice made possible.

Just as God put Jesus in the world to redeem it, He put you in the world to take the gospel to those who need to hear it. Name three girls you know who still have not found the eternal peace you have found. Beside each name, list one way you can show them the gentleness of Jesus.

Spend some time talking to God. Tell Him what you think makes Jesus' gentleness so remarkable and what you believe He expects from you as someone who continues to benefit from Jesus' gentleness. Thank God for the opportunity to show others the gentleness Jesus showed you.

Poured Out

DAY 3

LOSS AND BLESSING

discover

READ MATTHEW 5:3-12.

Blessed are the humble, for they will inherit the earth.
—Matthew 5:5

Jesus' sacrifice began long before His crucifixion. To become the great High Priest we needed, Jesus exchanged the glory of heaven for the struggle of earth. He understood much better than we do how far we all fell when Adam sinned.

In His Sermon on the Mount, Jesus listed the attributes of those God blesses. None are traits the world champions, but they are necessary for those who want to experience God. The key to possessing them is not in trying harder, but in allowing God to open our eyes. Until we see our sin and its consequences clearly, we can't and won't let God meet our need. When God shows us who we are and where we stand without His help, we are able and likely to accept His grace.

Those who accept God's grace are filled with gratitude that changes the way they think and act. God's glory becomes more important to them than anything else; they become selfless servants who communicate God's worth to the world—the kind Jesus described in Matthew 5:5. God blesses them, and His blessing outweighs any reward this world has to offer.

God is holy and is worthy of worship. Worshiping Him is that much sweeter—and a blessing in itself—because God loves us and sent Jesus to rescue us.

delight

Whom do you know who possesses the qualities Jesus listed in the Sermon on the Mount?

How does the world typically respond to people who possess these qualities?

display

Go back through today's reading and note the qualities of those Jesus said are blessed. In your Bible, next to each one, write the name of a girl or woman who possesses that quality. Consider how the world treats each of these girls or women and the eternal impact of their testimony. Determine whether or not the sacrifices they make are worth the cost.

As you go about your day, consider whether or not you possess any or all of the qualities Jesus listed and what the presence or absence of these qualities says about your relationship to and with God.

Talk to God about what you read today. Even if you have already put your faith in Jesus, ask God to show you who you would be without His constant help. Confess your sin and thank Him for His forgiveness. Ask God to develop in you the attributes Jesus listed.

Poured Out

DAY 4

LIVING PROOF

READ TITUS 3:1-7.

*Remind them to submit to rulers and authorities, to obey, to be
ready for every good work, to slander no one, to avoid fighting,
and to be kind, always showing gentleness to all people.*
—*Titus 3:1-2*

In his letter to Titus, a young man he had personally led to faith in
Jesus, the apostle Paul gave instructions for Christians who were
just learning how to live set apart by and for God. Paul's letter dealt
with interpersonal relationships both inside and outside the church,
which is made up of everyone who has put their faith in the gospel
of Jesus for salvation.

The only thing that sets children of God apart from everyone else
is the Holy Spirit's presence. It is our responsibility as daughters of
God to let the Holy Spirit shine through us by obeying God in the
details like the ones Paul described. When we do, we give those
around us reason to believe we really have been made new; we
encourage them to put their faith in the gospel of Jesus, too.

Nothing compares to the thrill of knowing God, but we must
be careful to never let what He is doing in and through us go to
our head or to take credit for it. After all, until we met Jesus, we
were just like everyone else. This should stir gentleness in us, not
arrogance. Prideful Christians lead others to believe God's grace
only extends to some, but gentle Christians grow His kingdom.

delight

What does the way you interact with people say to them about your relationship with God?

Does the way you treat people make the gospel of Jesus more or less appealing to those who know you believe it?

display

Name a girl you come in contact with regularly who seems to bring out the worst in you. Write out at least one of the actions steps given in today's key verse that you can practice when you interact with her.

Thank God for setting you free from a life characterized by sin. Thank Him for the Holy Spirit's presence and power in your life. Ask Him to give you opportunities to practice gentleness so others will want to know Him as you do. Commit to follow through when He does.

SEIZING OPPORTUNITY

discover

READ 1 PETER 3:13-17.

But in your hearts, regard Christ the Lord as holy, ready at any time to give a defense to anyone who asks you for a reason for the hope that is in you. Yet do this with gentleness and reverence, keeping a clear conscience, so that when you are accused, those who disparage your good conduct in Christ will be put to shame.
—1 Peter 3:15-16

When people treat children of God badly for doing good, injustice becomes opportunity. Most people are nice to nice people and mean to mean people, but the Holy Spirit helps children of God respond to meanness with gentleness. This makes others curious. When people ask about our response, we must be ready to speak the truth of the gospel.

People need to know that Jesus, the Son of God, conquered sin and death once and for all, set us free through faith, and made us new by the power of the Holy Spirit. They need to know we are citizens of God's kingdom and submit to and love others because God told us to. Furthermore, they need to know they can be saved.

Some people get agitated when the Holy Spirit reveals truth, but we must be careful not to distract or stir doubt by responding in kind. All authority in heaven and on earth belonged to Jesus, but He did not hold it over people. He simply spoke the truth with gentleness and reverence and left the rest up to God. We must do the same.

delight

What must you believe before you can see opportunity in suffering?

Where in your typical daily interaction with people do you see potential for opportunities to display gentleness in the face of difficulty or meanness directed at you?

display

Consider the way people have responded to you over the past couple of weeks. Identify opportunities God has given you to prove the presence of the Holy Spirit in your life by being gentle to others. Evaluate the ways you have handled those opportunities, consider what you could have done better, and plan what you will do next time God gives you a similar opportunity.

Write out a short script you could use to share the gospel when people wonder how you manage to be nice to mean people.

Think about the girls around you who aren't always kind and gentle. Write out their names, thank God for them, and commit to praying for them to come to know Jesus and His gentleness this month.

Talk to God for a while. Thank Him for helping you rise above meanness by the power of His Holy Spirit and for the privilege of sharing the gospel of Jesus. Ask Him to give you more opportunities to stir curiosity through gentleness so you can share it more often.

Poured Out

"Come to me, all of you who are weary and burdened, and I will give you rest. Take up my yoke and learn from me, because I am lowly and humble in heart, and you will find rest for your souls. For my yoke is easy and my burden is light."

MATTHEW 11:28-30

DAY 6

THE POWER OF A GENTLE RESPONSE

discover

READ PROVERBS 15:1-2.

A gentle answer turns away anger, but a harsh word stirs up wrath.
—Proverbs 15:1

It's impossible to avoid conflict. Sooner or later, someone will get frustrated or angry with us, and when that happens, we must not forget whose we are or the mission that is ours as His children. As we follow Jesus, our top priority must always be to seek and save the lost for the glory of our heavenly Father.

Because no other cause is as important as this one, no opinion we could hold or argument we want to win is as important as representing God's character well, even under pressure. Although He, being holy God, is entitled to express His righteous wrath when appropriate, we are not. Instead, we must focus on reflecting His gentleness in all situations.

When the Holy Spirit begins to draw those who do not know God to repentance, they often look for reasons to resist. We must not give them a reason by losing our tempers or using harsh words. Nothing must compete with the gospel of Jesus Christ. We can't express concern for our own opinions and ideas over the ultimate purpose of God's glory. When we manage conflict with gentleness, we prove the gospel powerful to save and transform and make it attractive to those who are searching like we once were. We offer relief and hope rather than stirring the pot.

delight

What are your natural conversational tendencies when confronted by a girl who is frustrated or angry with you?

What could you change to better reflect God's gentleness and the gospel's power to save and transform?

display

Think about the girl(s) you most often have confrontational conversations with and the reason they typically become confrontational. With Jesus as your example, prioritize her needs over your own. Decide that, from now on, you will not allow conversations with her to devolve into anything she could use as an excuse not to listen to the Holy Spirit or to dismiss the gospel of Jesus.

Prepare a sentence that you could use to diffuse tension when conflict arises in future conversations with this girl.

Spend some time talking to God. Confess any confrontational tendencies you may have that fail to reveal God's gentleness to those around you or prove the gospel powerful. Ask God to help you see through people's behavior to their needs and to respond to them with patience and compassion, avoiding harsh words.

DAY 7

CLEARING THE PATH

READ 2 TIMOTHY 2:22-26.

*The Lord's servant must not quarrel, but be gentle to
everyone, able to teach, and patient, instructing his
opponents with gentleness. Perhaps God will grant them
repentance leading them to a knowledge of the truth.*
—2 Timothy 2:24-25

With spiritual maturity comes the realization that life is not about
us. God creates us for His glory, saves us for His glory, and uses
us to save others for His glory as well. The more completely we
cooperate with the Holy Spirit in this pursuit, the more complete
our joy and satisfaction in life will be.

Once we recognize and learn to value conversations for the
opportunity it provides to glorify God, we will stop wasting words
on temporary concerns and start using them to build what lasts
forever—God's kingdom. Instead of trying to impress people and
win arguments, we will look for opportunities to teach by speaking
the truth of God's Word so the Holy Spirit can then use our words
to speak to hearts and draw people toward Him.

With our hearts purified from selfishness by the power of the
Holy Spirit, we will no longer take pleasure in shaming those who
challenge us, but rejoice when God is able to use our gentle
attitude and intentional efforts to rescue them. We will stop getting
in the way of salvation and encourage others to repentance by our
own example for His glory.

delight

What does the way you typically interact with people communicate about God and the importance of salvation through His Son Jesus?

How would your making His kingdom the goal of all conversations change the way you talk to others?

display

Write out what you believe God wants all of His children to value and accomplish in conversation with others. Name three ways you can succeed in this aim in your conversations this week.

Thank God for letting you participate in other people's lives. Ask Him to forgive you for wasting conversations with them that could have been spent on His purposes. Ask Him to help you recognize opportunities to speak the truth of His Word and commit to take advantage of those opportunities for His glory.

Poured Out

DAY 8

GENTLENESS AND GODLY WISDOM

discover

READ JAMES 3:13-18.

*Who among you is wise and understanding? By his
good conduct he should show that his works are done
in the gentleness that comes from wisdom.*
—James 3:13

Biblical wisdom is the knowledge of God applied. Those who have
found salvation through the gospel of Jesus come to understand
God's holiness, power, and sovereignty, and they experience
for themselves His goodness, grace, and mercy. Their intimate
knowledge of God stirs gratitude in their hearts and compels them
to reflect His character with the Holy Spirit's help.

A believers' relationship with God leads to wisdom. Wisdom has
markers in a believer's life. James mentioned a few of these in
verse 17—purity, loving peace, gentleness, compliance, mercy,
dependability, and an authenticity that can't be faked. These things
are the fruit of a life filled with God's wisdom.

Those who do not know God display worldly wisdom. Enslaved
by selfish ambition and jealousy, they deny God's provision and
character with their actions. They serve their own purposes, and
their actions cause confusion and stir conflict, creating the perfect
environment for evil to thrive and bring harm to themselves and
to others. Only when they finally put their faith in the gospel of
Jesus for salvation will they find the peace they crave and begin to
display the kind of wisdom that comes from knowing God.

delight

Do you typically do and say things to promote, preserve, and prosper yourself or God's kingdom? Explain.

What does your attitude and behavior say about your personal knowledge of God's wisdom?

display

List the places where you spend most of your time.

Examine your heart. What type of presence do you bring to these environments? Do you supply godly wisdom or worldly wisdom? Using today's reading as a reference, identify any changes you need to make going forward to be a source of gentleness and godly wisdom.

Thank God for the peace you have found in Him through Jesus and for the privilege of displaying godly wisdom in a self-centered world. Ask Him to use your gentleness to show the world who He is and what He can do in a surrendered heart.

DAY 9

RESPONSIBLE TO RESTORE

discover

READ GALATIANS 6:1-5.

*Brothers and sisters, if someone is overtaken in any wrongdoing,
you who are spiritual, restore such a person with a gentle spirit,
watching out for yourselves so that you also won't be tempted. Carry
one another's burdens; in this way, you will fulfill the law of Christ.*
—Galatians 6:1-2

When another girl messes up, we are sometimes tempted to pass judgment on her and get puffed up with pride. Clearly, this type of behavior does not honor God. The truth is, as long as we live in these flesh-and-bone bodies, we will all continue to struggle with sin—even after we have been set free from its consequences through faith in Jesus. This being true, none of us have the right to pass judgment on others or gloat.

Instead, we should rely on the Holy Spirit's help to restore sisters who make mistakes. The goal of this restoration is not improved behavior for our sake, but communion with God. No one is more miserable than a child of God who is not keeping in step with the Spirit. We restore others by pointing out their mistakes with gentleness, explaining what makes their actions wrong, and demonstrating what to do instead.

Restoration takes time, but it is our job to help one another out of reverence for God. When we share each other's burdens, we demonstrate His love; when we do so with humility, we demonstrate an understanding of who He is and who we are not.

delight

How do you typically respond when you see or hear about a godly girl who has fallen into sin?

Why do you suppose gentleness is so crucial to the restoration process?

display

Think of some of the mistakes you've made since putting your faith in Jesus. Consider how the girls around you responded to your mistakes and how their responses affected your desire to get back in step with the Holy Spirit. Identify the girls who were helpful and determine what made their attempts at restoration successful.

Use their example to make a list of helpful tips for others who want to be just as successful when restoring one another.

Spend some time with God. Thank Him for being patient with your mistakes and for sending sisters in Christ to restore you when needed. Ask Him for opportunities to help restore other Christian girls with gentleness.

DAY 10

SOMETHING IN COMMON

READ EPHESIANS 4:1-6.

*Therefore I, a prisoner in the Lord, urge you to walk worthy of
the calling you have received, with all humility and gentleness,
with patience, bearing with one another in love, making every
effort to keep the unity of the Spirit through the bond of peace.
There is one body and one Spirit—just as you were called to one
hope at your calling—one Lord, one faith, one baptism, one God
and Father of all, Who is above all and through all and in all.
—Ephesians 4:1-3*

Although some might have used being in prison as an excuse
to slack off, Paul used it to reveal his commitment to the calling
of God on his life. God desires the same from us, no matter our
circumstances. We will never be worthy of salvation through our
own efforts. However, through the salvation we receive from God
and the power of the Holy Spirit, we can live in a manner worthy
of it.

Although we benefit from it, the ultimate goal of the gospel of
Jesus is God's glory, not our comfort. This being true, we must
make every effort to make sure God gets this glory by pursuing
unity over individual interest.

When we—as naturally selfish people who should be at odds—
exercise patience and display gentleness with one another instead,
we prove the presence of the Holy Spirit at work in our lives as a
result of the gospel. This leaves those who would like to reject the
gospel without an excuse to do so.

delight

What evidence can you provide that reflects you are willing to make "every effort to keep the unity of the Spirit" among your sisters in Jesus?

What comfort can you draw from the fact that the same Spirit who lives in you lives in every child of God?

display

Think about the people you know who claim to know Jesus. Identify any conflict or discord that exists among them. Determine what you can do in each situation to "keep the unity of the Spirit" and purpose to do it. Using today's reading as a guide, on a separate piece of paper, list objectives to keep in mind when you interact with other girls who are part of the body of Christ, the global church. Post or store this list where you will find it often and be reminded.

Thank God for calling you to salvation and obedience and for sisters who have the same Holy Spirit inside. Thank God for the mutual understanding this provides when you interact with them. Commit to put individual interests aside in pursuit of unity for His glory.

A GENTLE RESPONSE

We often hear that we won't know how to respond unless we're actually in a certain situation. While that might be true to an extent—we can't see the future and don't know what exact actions we'll take—we can prepare our hearts to respond well by knowing God, using His wisdom, and listening to the Holy Spirit's guidance to respond in any situation.

Read each of the following scenarios, then think about how you would respond. Then notice how Jesus responded to similar situations.

Ava's best friend, Mel, promised to always be there for her. Ava shared all of her deepest feelings with Mel—all of her secrets. But when some of the popular girls from school decided to turn on Ava because of her beliefs, Mel pretended like she didn't even know her.

Kaylee and Angelina are best friends who decide to have some other friends over to hang out. Kaylee is stressing over every little detail—constantly restocking the chips and salsa, making sure everyone has a water bottle, grabbing all the cozy blankets. She basically misses most of the night because she's trying to make sure everyone else is having a good time. Halfway through the night, she stops, turns to Angelina, and snaps: "Why are you not helping me? Don't you think I'd like to have fun too?!"

There are some girls at school who constantly pick on a girl named Gracie. They gossip about her constantly, spreading lies around the school. They've pushed her books out of her hands in the hallway. They've shamed her and called her out on social media. And one of the girls even slapped her and called her a name.

Nevaeh's best friend is a bit impulsive and super protective. Someone said something mean and untrue about her friend, Vanessa, online. She commented in Vanessa's defense, berating the other girl for being so awful.

Jada ordered her go-to drink at her favorite coffee shop and realized she had left her purse in the car. The girl behind her paid for her drink. She turned to thank her and realized it was her favorite celebrity. They even sat down together and chatted for a minute. Jada shyly asked for a picture, and she agreed. Jada called her friends as soon as she left to tell them the good news. But they didn't believe her until she showed them the photo at school the next day.

Read Luke 22:54-62; John 21:15-19. Does anything about Jesus' response change the way you'd respond if you were Ava? Explain.

Read Luke 10:38-42. Does anything about Jesus' response change the way you'd respond if you were Angelina? Explain.

Read Luke 23:33-34; John 19:1-16. Does anything about Jesus' response change the way you'd respond if you were Gracie? Explain.

Read Luke 22:49-51. Does anything about Jesus' response change the way you'd respond if you were Nevaeh? Explain.

Read Luke 24:13-35. Does anything about Jesus' response change the way you'd respond if you were Jada? Explain.

Jesus' responses in these scenarios (and many others) might seem unusual to us.

- Jesus forgave one of His closest friends, Peter, as many times as Peter had originally denied Him.
- Jesus pointed out to Martha that it was OK to sit with her guests instead of spending the whole visit working to make sure the guests were cared for.
- Jesus asked the Father to forgive the very people who crucified Him.
- Jesus healed the arresting priest's servant harmed by one of His disciples in Gethsemane.
- Jesus patiently revealed the truth to His disciples in the midst of their fear (and unbelief) after His resurrection, even though He had told them all of these things would happen.

In every one of these scenarios, and throughout His ministry, Jesus shows us how to respond to difficult people and circumstances with gentleness, love, and grace. While you won't experience the exact difficulties Jesus did, learning these biblical accounts of how Jesus handled adversity can show you exactly how to do the same. Learn from His example, and lead others by your own.

DAY 11

PRAYER AND GENTLENESS

discover

READ PHILIPPIANS 4:4-7.

Let your graciousness be known to everyone. The Lord is near.
Don't worry about anything, but in everything, through prayer
and petition with thanksgiving, present your requests to God.
And the peace of God, which surpasses all understanding,
will guard your hearts and minds in Christ Jesus.
—Philippians 4:5–7

Things do not always go the way we want them to, and people don't always act the way we want them to act, but that is no reason to alter the way we live our lives. When we get frustrated, children of God must make a conscious choice to focus on what God has done for us and celebrate it by loving others.

To be gracious is to treat people better than they deserve, and gentleness is a form of grace. Because God is gracious, we must be gentle. Worry gets in the way of this sometimes, but there is a cure for worry: prayer. When we lay all our worries at God's feet, He takes care of the things we are tempted to fix ourselves—situations and people—and settles our hearts so we can focus on how we treat people instead of how we wish things were.

The more consistent our prayer lives, the more peaceful and inclined to show grace we become. Why? Because God changes our hearts through prayer. Our reputation for gentleness marks us as children of God and advances His kingdom. That gives us plenty of reason to rejoice!

delight

What wishes and worries tend to get in the way of your being gentle with other people?

Name a girl you know who has a reputation for gentleness. How does she glorify God with her words, actions, and attitude?

display

List three situations in your life that you wish were different.

For each, consider the motivation behind your desire for it to be different. Cross out each wish that is driven by selfish motives and circle those that are driven by the desire to see God glorified.

Now make a list of things you know to be true about God.

Compare your lists and determine how God might be able to glorify Himself in each circled instance if you pray, leave it with Him, and focus on gentleness.

Spend some time talking to God about what has been frustrating you lately. Tell Him who you believe Him to be and what you believe Him to be capable of. Ask Him to glorify Himself in each situation and promise not to interfere, but to focus instead on being gentle.

Poured Out

DAY 12

PROVING GOD'S STRENGTH

discover

READ ISAIAH 40:10-11.

See, the LORD comes with strength, and his power establishes his rule.
His wages are with him, and his reward accompanies him. He protects
his flock like a shepherd; he gathers the lambs in his arms and carries
them in the fold of his garment. He gently leads those that are nursing.

The world tells us we must dominate others to prove we are strong
and take from others to get rich, but God sets a different example
and calls His children to a higher standard.

Almighty, sovereign God is both prosperous and powerful. The
world and everything in it is His, and nothing is impossible for Him.
However, these truths do not keep Him from being gentle with
us or seeing to our needs. On the contrary, He is able to invest in
us without diminishing Himself or His resources in any way, so His
gentle care proves His strength. Because God's riches are abundant
beyond imagining, He is able to bless us accordingly.

When we follow God's example and rely on His provision to
show gentleness to all, we tell the world we have nothing more
important to do than love others because God has already met our
needs. We prove His grace to be sufficient and bring Him glory.

delight

When and how has God shown you gentleness?

How can you help others understand that God is both all powerful and gentle and that these two attributes do not contradict each other?

display

Recall times in your life when you were vulnerable and needy. Consider how God used other girls to show you gentleness and provide for your needs. On a sticky note, make a list of girls who blessed you during those times. Write thank you notes to two or more of those girls, telling them how their gentleness affected your life and what they taught you about God.

Thank God for being strong and providing for you, naming specific instances. Thank Him for people who have relied on His provision to show you gentleness and ask Him for the opportunity to show that same gentleness to others so they will believe He is strong and trust Him.

Poured Out

DAY 13

PUTTING ON GENTLENESS

discover

READ COLOSSIANS 3:12-17.

Therefore, as God's chosen ones, holy and dearly loved,
put on compassion, kindness, humility, gentleness, and
patience, bearing with one another and forgiving one
another if anyone has a grievance against another. Just as
the Lord has forgiven you, so you also are to forgive.
—Colossians 3:12

When we put our faith in the gospel of Jesus, God sanctifies us—or sets us apart—for Himself once and for all. This is called positional sanctification. Even so, there is work to be done. Although the Holy Spirit makes us new the moment we put our faith in Jesus, it takes a while for us to look and act like Him because this transformation requires our cooperation.

When we partner with the Holy Spirit through intentional obedience to God's Word, the Bible, we start to think, sound, and act differently than those who do not know Jesus. This sets us apart and is called experiential sanctification.

Gentleness is one of God's attributes. The Bible tells us to "put it on" so that we will look like Him and give the world a glimpse of His character, so we must make an intentional effort to do so. As we work to be gentle, the Holy Spirit provides us with the ability, God moves through us, and we learn more about Him. Our gratitude overflows, and our desire to make Him known spills over in service to others, resulting in His glory.

delight

On a scale from one to ten, where would you rank your level of cooperation with the Holy Spirit in the pursuit of Christ-likeness? Explain.

Where does gentleness rank in degree of difficulty for you among the attributes listed in verse 12? Why?

display

Consider the difference being set apart by and for God has made in your life and what He deserves in return. Go back through all of the attributes and actions listed in today's passage. Choose five or six, including gentleness, and think of practical ways you can display these attributes or complete these actions in the next twenty-four hours. Make a to-do list for yourself and check off each goal as you complete it.

Thank God for setting you apart for Himself when you put your faith in the gospel of Jesus and for the privilege of reflecting His character. Commit to cooperate with the Holy Spirit when He guides and empowers you to obey God so you can look more like Jesus.

DAY 14

PURSUING GENTLENESS

READ 1 TIMOTHY 6:3-12.

But you, man of God, flee from these things, and pursue
righteousness, godliness, faith, love, endurance, and gentleness.
—1 Timothy 6:11

These days, everyone has an opinion, and no one has to earn their voice. It can be difficult to discern what is true and whom to trust. God has given us the Bible—His inspired Word recorded by men— to serve as the ultimate authority on all matters, but people have become skilled at twisting its words. The only way to know for sure whether something is true is to study God's Word ourselves, and the only way to know for sure whether a person can be trusted is to study their behavior.

Academic knowledge of God's Word does not prove personal knowledge of God. People who thrive on conflict, work to impress people with what they know, and/or exploit the gospel for personal gain are arrogant, and arrogance proves spiritual ignorance. Those who know God well serve Him only. Those who serve themselves don't know God well enough to be trusted.

God expects His children to "fight the good fight," yes, but this fight requires faith, not aggression. When we face conflict, we must meet it as Jesus did: with righteousness, godliness, faith, love, endurance, and gentleness. God has given us eternal life through His Son, and nothing argues this truth more powerfully than our determination to enjoy it now through obedience to His Word, regardless of what others think or say.

delight

What is your typical response when confronted by someone who wants to argue about spiritual matters? How might your response need to change?

What changes do you think we would see in the world if every child of God followed the instructions given in today's passage?

display

Consider how the people in your life typically interact with one another and what their words, actions, and attitudes reveal about whom they serve. Understanding that no one is perfect and reserving judgment, consider whether or not the people you normally listen to have actually earned your trust in spiritual matters.

Next, consider the way you typically interact with others and what your words, actions, and attitudes reveal about who you serve. Make a list of things that need to change.

Thank God for making you new and giving you eternal life through faith in the gospel of Jesus so you no longer have to endure the strife that comes with serving yourself. Thank Him for faithful examples of godliness to follow in a world that promotes conflict and commit to being an example.

DAY 15

GOD'S GENTLE WHISPER

discover

READ 1 KINGS 19:11-13a.

After the earthquake there was a fire, but the LORD was not in the fire. And after the fire, there was a voice, a soft whisper.
—1 Kings 19:12

Elijah was a faithful prophet. Through him, God performed life-altering miracles to glorify Himself—the kind of miracles we long to be a part of, or at least witness with our own eyes. Having been created by God with a capacity to know Him, we crave the awesome, but spectacle is not what we need most.

If anyone understood this, it was Elijah. On the run from Jezebel for his part in a public display of God's power, Elijah grew so discouraged he wanted to die. But God comforted Him. When God came near, the cliffs shattered, an earthquake shook the ground, and the land caught fire. But these side-effects of God's nearness did nothing to soothe the soul of God's faithful servant, who had already seen it all, so to speak. Only when God whispered did Elijah recognize God's presence.

God sometimes chooses to speak through the kind of miracles that make good bedtime stories, but if we spend all our energy and time watching for God to reveal Himself in this way, we could miss the greatest miracle of all—the voice of the great I AM gently speaking directly to our hearts. Shock and awe fade with memory, but the joy of communion with God lasts forever.

delight

What was the last miracle from God you experienced or witnessed? How did it affect you?

What was the last thing God whispered to your heart? How did it affect you?

display

Using the heading "What I want for and from God," make a list of things you are asking God to do in your life and in the lives of those around you. Then, using the heading "What God wants for and from me," make a list of things God has whispered to your heart recently. Compare the length of your two lists and what it implies about your listening skills where God is concerned. For the rest of the day, focus on hearing God's voice for the purpose of adding to your second list.

What I Want for/from God   **What God Wants for/from Me**

Thank God for the privilege of knowing Him and for speaking to you in a variety of ways. Ask Him to open your eyes to His activity around you and to train your heart to hear His voice. Commit to listen when He speaks, meditate on His Word, and respond appropriately.

Poured Out

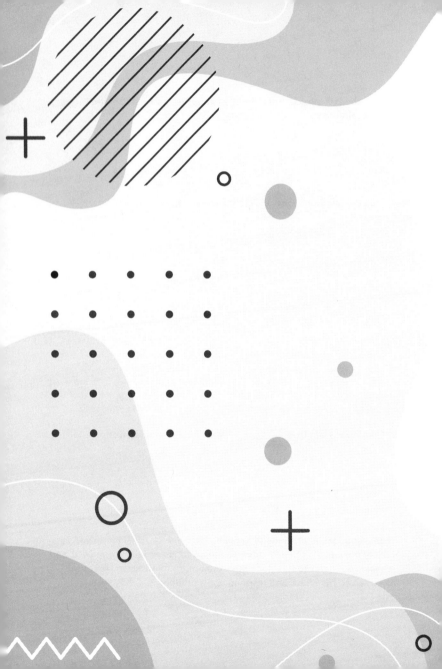

Adopt the same attitude as that of Christ Jesus,

who, existing in the form of God,

did not consider equality with God

as something to be exploited.

Instead he emptied himself

by assuming the form of a servant,

taking on the likeness of humanity.

And when he had come as a man,

he humbled himself by becoming obedient

to the point of death—

even to death on a cross.

PHILIPPIANS 2:5-8

DAY 16

JESUS' GENTLE LEADERSHIP

discover

READ MARK 10:35-45.

Jesus called them over and said to them, "You know that those who are regarded as rulers of the Gentiles lord it over them, and those in high positions act as tyrants over them. But it is not so among you. On the contrary, whoever wants to become great among you will be your servant, and whoever wants to be first among you will be a slave to all. For even the Son of Man did not come to be served, but to serve, and to give His life as a ransom for many."
—Mark 10:42-45

Human nature craves glory and recognition, but those who have given their lives to Jesus forfeit such things. Like Jesus, they seek to serve not to better themselves or make themselves seem saintly, but so others would see God's hand at work in their lives. Those who have given their lives to Christ also recognize His willingness and ability to save and transform. Christians praise Him for the change He brings in others and long for people to trust Him with their lives.

Through gentle service, Jesus was able to do so much more in service of God's kingdom than any of the vain and brutish rulers of His day were able to do for themselves. The same is true today for those who follow Jesus' example and serve others with gentleness.

delight

How do children of God who abuse the authority God gave them or serve with selfish motives instead of demonstrating gentleness for God's glory endanger our shared mission to introduce people to Jesus?

When have you been tempted to abuse your authority or serve with selfish motives?

display

We are called to serve others for God's glory alone, but God does bless us when we serve.

Make a list of ways you have served over the past year.

Next to each, write down any blessings you received from God as a result of your service. Then, go back through your list and examine the motivation behind each act of service. Consider how the motivation behind your service affected the level of gentleness you displayed.

> **Thank God for the privilege of serving others in His name. Thank Him for using your service to build His eternal kingdom. Ask Him to give you a deeper desire to see Him glorified and help you recognize opportunities to serve others with gentleness when they happen.**

DAY 17

JESUS' GENTLE SERVICE

discover

READ JOHN 13:3-11.

So he got up from supper, laid aside his outer clothing, took a towel, and tied it around himself. Next, he poured water into a basin and began to wash his disciples' feet and to dry them with the towel tied around him.
—John 13:4-5

Jesus sat down to the last supper knowing He was about to be arrested and crucified. So His disciples would not miss the significance of what was about to happen or how they should respond, Jesus washed their feet.

Peter objected. Whether Peter's objection had more to do with his love and respect for Jesus or wounded pride at the thought of his own master serving others, we do not know. But we do know that Peter was willing to let Jesus wash his feet once he realized it was the only way he could have a relationship with Him. Later, with his very soul washed clean through faith in Jesus' death and resurrection, Peter went on to serve others in the same way Jesus did. He was eventually martyred.

All authority in heaven and earth was given to Jesus, and He used it to serve and save. We like to focus on the saving part—the cross was an admirable act of heroism by anyone's standards—but we can't ignore the serving part and fulfill our God-given purpose. Like Peter, we must be willing to perform whatever act of service obedience requires—heroic or mundane—with gentleness after Jesus' example.

delight

Which acts of service do you typically resist performing? Why?

Why is it important not only to serve others in whatever way God requires, but to do so with the same gentleness and humility Jesus displayed?

display

Do two things today. First, use a blank sheet of paper to record acts of service you see other girls perform. When you have time to sit and reflect, consider the attitude with which each girl performed her act of service. Put a star next to the acts of service you believe glorified God most and explain why.

Second, look for God-given opportunities to serve. Observe your own willingness or reluctance to obey God and consider the reason(s) for any reluctance you feel. When you have time to reflect, identify areas of your heart you need to let God work on.

Thank God for Jesus' sacrifice and example of humility and gentleness in service. Ask God to give you opportunities to serve in ways that challenge you. Commit to follow through with a grateful heart.

DAY 18

JESUS' GENTLE ATTITUDE

READ PHILIPPIANS 2:3-11.

Adopt the same attitude as Christ Jesus, who, existing in the form of God, did not consider equality with God as something to be exploited. Instead, he emptied himself by assuming the form of a servant, taking on the likeness of humanity. And when he had come as a man, he humbled himself by becoming obedient to the point of death—even to death on a cross.
—*Philippians 2:5-8*

Before a person can become a child of God, they must see their need for a Savior. They must know in their heart they are spiritually bankrupt and cannot buy themselves out of slavery to sin. To be rescued, they must put their faith in the gospel of Jesus by surrendering control of their lives to Him. They must lay aside their own will and purposes and take up His.

Unfortunately, some of God's children forget over time that they are just sinners like everyone else—sinners saved by grace. Instead of showing proper humility before God and appropriate gratitude for their salvation by serving others, they begin to think more of themselves than they should and sometimes use their status as children of God for personal gain. This is a sad state for a believer.

Jesus is God. If anyone was entitled to use His status for personal gain, He was. But He forfeited those rights on earth and served others. Those who follow Him must adopt the same attitude, serving with the same gentleness and for the same purpose.

delight

Why is it so important for those who do not know God yet to see God's children giving instead of taking and promoting God instead of themselves?

Does the way that you typically interact with others display a proper understanding of who and where you would be without God? Explain.

display

Make a mark that no one but you would notice on your hand where you will see it throughout the day. Every time you see this mark, take notice of your words, actions, and attitude, and consider whether you are promoting self or God to those around you. Make immediate adjustments when and where necessary.

At the end of the day, spend some time reflecting on what you noticed and what it indicates about the condition of your heart. Write yourself a letter of correction and encouragement to keep in your Bible for future reference.

Thank God for sending His Son Jesus to redeem you from slavery to sin. Thank God for the privilege of becoming His child forever. Ask Him to get your attention when you start to get puffed up or selfish so you can adjust your attitude to match Jesus'.

DAY 19

JESUS' GENTLE WELCOME

discover

READ LUKE 18:15-17.

Jesus, however, invited them: "Let the little children come to me, and don't stop them, because the kingdom of God belongs to such as these. Truly I tell you, whoever does not receive the kingdom of God like a little child will never enter it."
—Luke 18:16-17

The Bible tells us that God draws people to Himself. It is no more up to us than it was up to Jesus' disciples to decide who should or should not get to be a part of what God was doing. If we ever find ourselves making such judgment calls, we can assume we have lost sight of what the gospel did in us and what it can do in others. Before moving forward, we must stop, let the Holy Spirit search our hearts, and repent of any arrogance or prejudice He finds, because such attitudes hinder the advancement of God's kingdom.

God does not want us to make decisions for Him; He wants to decide for us. Our job is to stay open and obedient. If we continue in the childlike faith we showed when we were first saved, He will keep showing Himself to us and make us more like Jesus— who, thankfully, is willing to receive all of us just as we are. Our interactions with others will show gentleness, and those who are looking for Jesus will come to us to be introduced, knowing they will not be turned away.

delight

What do your best friends or other godly girls you know tell the world about the availability of salvation through Jesus?

Is your service to God's kingdom marked by stubbornness and willpower or commitment to God's purposes and complete dependence on Him? Explain.

display

Before you live out your day, think through the paths your feet will walk, the directions they typically take, and the people they typically lead you to. Consider whether your steps are usually decided by God according to His plan or by your agenda according to what you think you need.

Name three people you have been ignoring even though you know God wants you to talk to them. Take time to talk to and listen to them today.

Thank God for giving you the faith you needed to become His child. Ask Him to remind you to keep walking in that faith so you do not miss what He wants to do in your life and in the lives of those around you.

Poured Out

DAY 20

JESUS' GENTLE REVELATION

discover

READ JOHN 4:1-26.

*"Go call your husband," he told her, "and come back here." "I don't
have a husband," she answered. "You have correctly said, 'I don't have
a husband,'" Jesus said. "For you've had five husbands, and the man
you now have is not your husband. What you have said is true."*
—John 4:16-18

On His way to Galilea through Samaria, Jesus met a Samaritan
woman at a well while He waited for His disciples to return with
food. At that time, the Jews considered Samaritans unclean
because of their mixed Gentile blood. Not only was this woman
considered an outcast by the Jews, but she was also probably
an outcast among her own people. We can guess this because
she chose to draw water when the rest of the women would not
be there.

As difficult as dealing with her social status may have been, the
Samaritan woman had a greater need. Like every other sinner,
she needed salvation from sin through Jesus. Knowing this, Jesus
didn't try to make her feel bad about her past, and He didn't try to
excuse her past mistakes. Instead, He cut straight to the truth of
her sin so she could see her need for a Savior. Then, He offered her
the rescue she needed. Jesus' gentleness made her want to listen.

God has not called us to make sinners feel better about their sin
or to berate and shame them for it. Instead, He has called us to
be ministers of reconciliation who bring light into darkness by
speaking the truth with gentleness.

delight

How does the way you usually communicate the truth of God's Word affect your audience's willingness to listen?

What is wrong with making people feel better about their sin?

display

Today, watch prayerfully for evidence of spiritual need in the words, actions, and attitudes of the girls around you. Instead of criticizing, judging, or holding them at arm's length, ask God to send someone to speak truth into their lives. Be ready for Him to send you.

At the end of the day, make a list of the girls you prayed for. Choose the girl you know best. Call, text, or write her a note to let her know you are praying for her and that she can always talk to you.

Thank God for everyone who has had the compassion and courage to speak the truth of God's Word into your life with gentleness. Ask God to use you like He has used them and to open your eyes to the spiritual needs of others.

GENTLE LIKE JESUS

To paint a verbal picture of a strong girl today, people often say she's: fierce, bold, strong, ambitious, a boss, independent, outspoken, and aggressive. She knows what she wants and she goes for it. She speaks her mind, and she does it well. She stands up for others and herself; she refuses to let people walk all over her.

What words and phrases would you use to describe a strong woman?

While these things aren't all bad or wrong, they aren't enough on their own. There's a flawed belief today that says holding back is weakness, tenderheartedness is weakness, being soft is weakness, gentleness is weakness. But in reality, gentleness is an in-between; it's a quiet and wise strength. Being gentle requires us to be bold, strong, and outspoken, but it also requires tenderness, compassion, and wisdom.

You do not have to be a doormat to be gentle and kind. Instead, you have to be like Jesus—the One who is identified as King and described as "gentle" in the very same verse (Matt. 21: 5). The One who promised "rest for [our] souls" because He is "gentle and lowly in heart" (Matt. 11:29, ESV). The One who welcomed the children, the women, the poor, the outsiders, and the sinners. The One who stood in opposition to law-based righteousness and the religious elite to offer grace, even as they accused Him of blasphemy and called Him a liar (see Matt. 26:57-68). The very same One who spoke truth and died for it—died for us. Jesus is the perfect example of gentleness.

So how do you know when it's good to let things go or to push back? How can you live in the gentle in-between?

- Speak the truth, but do it in love. Whether or not the person likes the truth you speak, when you speak gently and softly, you leave less room for anger (see Prov. 15:1; Eph. 4:15).
- Stand up for God and His Word (see Luke 23:50-56; Acts 6:8-7:53; 2 Tim. 4:2).
- Be bold in sharing the gospel and defending your faith (see Rom. 1:16; 1 Pet. 3:15).
- Serve in kindness and compassion the orphans, widows, poor, and the outsiders (see Lev. 19:33-34; Ps.82:3; 146:9; Prov. 19:17; Isa. 1:17; Luke 12:33; Col. 4:5).

- Be patient with those who don't understand or know the truth (see Luke 24:13-35; 2 Pet. 3:9).
- Seek justice for the oppressed (see Micah 6:8; Isa. 1:17).
- Pursue peace, not revenge. This includes freely offering forgiveness as we have been freely forgiven (see Matt. 6:14-15; Rom. 12:18-19; Eph. 4:32).
- Live out of a heart full of love for God, running after Him and loving others well (see Luke 10:27; 1 John 4:19).

PUT IT INTO PRACTICE

Describe how you can practice being gentle like Jesus in your own life.

It takes time to be gentle, to strike a balance between being a doormat or being too harsh. So, it's important to be gentle with yourself, too, as you grow in Christ. You won't live gently perfectly all the time, so remember that God forgives you when you mess up and confess it to Him (see 1 John 1:9). As you spend time in His Word and seek Him first in all things, you'll grow to be gentle like Jesus.

DAY 21

JESUS' GENTLE CORRECTION

READ JOHN 8:2-11.

When Jesus stood up, he said to her, "Woman, where are they? Has no one condemned you?" "No one, Lord," she answered. "Neither do I condemn you," said Jesus. "Go, and from now on, do not sin anymore."
—John 8:10-11

Everyone in the story of the woman caught in adultery had done something wrong…except Jesus. He could have judged them—He had the authority to do so—but He did not. Instead, Jesus showed mercy and grace by exposing the truth and letting the truth do its work in their hearts.

When He gave permission for anyone present who was without sin to throw the first stone, Jesus made everyone look inside themselves. He spared them the guilt of murdering a woman who was no worse than they were. When no one condemned the woman, Jesus didn't simply tell her to go on her way, but acknowledged the truth of the men's accusations and told her to leave her life of sin behind.

None of the people Jesus spoke to had the power to overcome their sin by themselves. They needed a Savior like Him; One with the power to condemn, but the desire to save. So do we. So do those around us. This being true, we must remember we are simply servants who still struggle with our sin nature, reveal the truth with gentleness, and let Him do His work without passing judgment or pretending salvation doesn't require repentance.

delight

What would your life be like if you had never repented of your sin and let Jesus rescue you?

How might your ability to minister to others' spiritual needs benefit from giving consideration to the previous question on a regular basis?

display

Today, work to see the girls around you as souls who need God instead of "good" or "bad" girls. Resist the temptation to decide for yourself what individual people deserve for what they have or have not done—that is God's job. Instead, heap grace and mercy on everyone. Speak the unbiased truth of God's Word with gentleness when He gives you the chance and encourage those around you to do the same.

When you have time to reflect, describe what happened and what you learned from it.

Thank God for correcting you when you need it so you can enjoy uninterrupted fellowship with Him. Ask Him to give you compassion for those whose sin is keeping them from experiencing Him. Ask Him to use you to guide them to peace with gentleness.

JESUS' GENTLE RESPONSE

discover

READ JOHN 11:28-44.

Jesus wept.
—John 11:35

The Bible says the fullness of God was in Jesus, so we can assume any attribute He displayed is also an attribute of God the Father. In today's passage, we witness Jesus' gentle compassion.

By the time Jesus arrived at His friend Lazarus' home, Lazarus had already been dead for four days. Jesus could have gotten to Lazarus quickly enough to save Him, but that's not what God wanted Him to do. Although no one told Him, Jesus knew the moment Lazarus died. Only when He came upon the mourners did He weep.

Jesus didn't weep for Lazarus; He knew He planned to raise Lazarus from the dead. Jesus didn't weep for Himself; it made no difference to Jesus what people thought He was or was not able to do. No, Jesus wept for His friends; it hurt Jesus to see people hurting, even thought He knew what was coming.

As Christ-followers, it's not our job to decide whether or not a person should be hurting, but to follow after Jesus's example in reflecting the character of God in our interactions with them. When we choose gentleness over judgment and mourn with those who mourn, we help them believe that the God we serve truly cares about what they are going through and wants to help.

delight

What determines how you respond when you find out someone is hurting?

How can God use the gentleness and compassion you show toward people who have caused their own grief for His glory?

display

Today, watch for girls who seem to be upset. Pray for them. Ask God to use what they are going through to make Himself known to them. When possible, smile, speak an encouraging word, and/or lighten their load if you can do so without encouraging behavior that does not honor God. When time and setting allow you to, ask if you can pray for them out loud and use that prayer to remind them God sees, God cares, and God can help.

Thank God for seeing you and knowing what you are going through at all times. Thank Him for having compassion on you and sending Jesus so you can experience peace and joy in all circumstances. Thank God for the privilege of showing this compassion to others.

DAY 23

JESUS' GENTLE ANGER

READ JOHN 2:13-16.

*After making a whip out of cords, he drove everyone out of the temple
with their sheep and oxen. He also poured out the money changers' coins
and overturned the tables. He told those who were selling doves, "Get these
things out of here! Stop turning my Father's house into a market place."*
—*John 2:15–16*

This passage is often used to excuse behavior that does not honor
God. When studying it, we must remember that Jesus was not only
a sinless human, but also God. We are neither. The righteous anger
Jesus displayed was His divine right; it's not ours.

We must also understand the reason for Jesus' anger. In His day,
it was common for people who didn't raise animals to buy their
sacrifices at the temple. They needed merchants. Jesus wasn't
angry because merchants were there, but because some sold
flawed animals, some charged too much, and many set up booths
where Gentiles worshiped.

Jesus' actions may seem violent, but He did show restraint. He
didn't wound or humiliate anyone and showed gentle concern for
worshipers. Jesus' actions may seem impulsive, but He only ever
did and said what God told Him to.

No less deserving of God's wrath than anyone else, we are first
and foremost reconcilers who deal in gentleness and should be
extremely skeptical of any calling we sense to "clear the temple"
ourselves. We proceed with caution, humility, and gentleness only
after much prayer and confirmation.

delight

What is the potential danger of claiming "righteous anger" when you are upset about something?

How can you mimic the gentle way Jesus confronted sin without flipping the switch to sinfully losing your temper?

display

Come up with a list of questions a person should ask themselves before acting in "righteous anger" or taking it upon themselves to punish or pass judgment on someone else. Today, watch how the girls around you show anger, paying careful attention to those who claim to follow Jesus. Keep track of your own anger, too, and record the outcome of all angry actions.

Use what you observed to make your list of questions more helpful. Keep it in your Bible.

Thank God for the mercy and grace He displays even in discipline. Ask God to help you care more about His reputation and the concerns of others than your own. Ask God to check you when you are tempted to show anger He has not given you permission to act on.

DAY 24

JESUS' GENTLE SUBMISSION

discover

READ JOHN 18:1-11.

Then Simon Peter, who had a sword, drew it, struck the high priest's
servant, and cut off his right ear. … At that, Jesus said to Peter, "Put
your sword away! Am I not to drink the cup the Father has given me?"
—John 18:10–11

When Jesus was arrested, He knew He was about to be crucified for the sins of humanity and raised on the third day. He had told His disciples this, but they were still caught off-guard. Peter reacted like many of us would; Jesus did not.

Jesus was more concerned about God's will being done than saving Himself. He showed extraordinary gentleness by not resisting arrest, not allowing His disciples to defend Him, healing the high priest's servant, and not shaming Judas, who had betrayed Him. Jesus' gentleness toward Judas was not new—Jesus had known what Judas would do back when He washed his feet—but Judas only became aware of it in this moment. The grief produced by Jesus' gentle response drove Judas to take his own life.

Human logic tells us if we can get Jesus-loving people to agree with, support, and/or defend our actions, we must be in the right—but this simply isn't true. Peter deeply loved Jesus, but he kept opposing God's plan, and Jesus kept having to correct him. We must always follow Jesus' example, only yielding to God's will and choosing gentleness over self-preservation for His glory.

delight

What does your typical response when you face opposition reveal about what you value most?

What does a Christ-follower's ability to respond with gentleness under pressure tell the world about the power of the gospel of Jesus?

display

Take a moment to consider what you will do if/when you face opposition today, considering the fact that God's glory is more important than self-preservation. Gentleness glorifies Him.

Make a list of action steps you will take if/when you are confronted.

Thank God for His gentleness toward you. Confess that your own plans often get in the way of His. Ask Him to stir in you a desire to see Him glorified that outweighs your desire to protect yourself. Commit to respond with gentleness when confronted.

Poured Out

DAY 25

JESUS' GENTLE PARDON

discover

READ LUKE 23:32-34.

Then Jesus said, "Father forgive them, because they do not know what they are doing." And they divided his clothes and cast lots.
—Luke 23:34

Forgiveness is not about feeling "okay" with someone; it is not about how we feel at all. Forgiveness is a financial term. To forgive someone is to forgive a debt. It's to believe and act as if a person no longer owes you. When Jesus asked God to forgive His crucifiers, He was literally asking God not to hold their actions against them.

God's children forgive because God has forgiven us and, in doing so, prove the existence of a supernatural Holy Spirit at work in our lives—present only as a result of our faith in the gospel of Jesus. We paint a picture of Jesus, the epitome of gentleness; the One who not only forgave, but also made forgiveness of sin possible before we even knew we needed it.

As Jesus spoke the words in today's key verse, the soldiers were still in the act of treating Him with disrespect. We must do the same, not only forgiving those who ask for it, but also forgiving those who don't know they need forgiveness and those who may know they need it, but don't care. After all, if what a person does to offend us really is sin, it's against God anyway, not us. Even if we are affected by their actions, we can let go and move on.

delight

Who is more affected by unforgiveness—the person who remains unforgiven or the person who refuses to forgive? Explain.

How might a child of God who refuses to forgive hinder God's plan in her life and the lives of those around her?

display

On a separate sheet of paper, do three things.

- First, name who has forgiven you when you didn't think you deserved it. Next to each name, write out what they forgave you for and how their forgiveness affected you.

- Second, name who you need to forgive. Next to each name, explain what you need to forgive them for and why.

- Third, decide these people no longer owe you, even if your interaction with them cannot stay the same or legal action must be taken for the sake of justice. Simply free your heart from the burden of hanging on to the wrong they committed against you.

Thank God for making a way for you to be forgiven through Jesus before you even knew you needed forgiveness. Commit to follow Jesus' gentle example by forgiving those whose sin affects you as soon as it happens, regardless of whether they know or care they hurt you.

Don't let anyone despise your
youth, but set an example for the
believers in speech, in conduct,
in love, in faith, and in purity.

1 TIMOTHY 4:12

JESUS' GENTLE RESTORATION

discover

READ JOHN 21:15-19.

> *He asked him the third time, "Simon, son of John, do you*
> *love me?" Peter was grieved that he asked him a third time,*
> *"Do you love me?" He said, "Lord, you know everything;*
> *you know that I love you." "Feed my sheep," Jesus said.*
> *—John 21:17-19*

In this conversation with Peter, Jesus restored Peter with gentleness and patience. Although Peter had sworn he would never deny Him, Jesus' arrest scared Peter, and he denied Jesus three times. Wanting desperately to make amends at this point, even though Jesus had already forgiven him, Peter was eager to express his love for the Lord.

On the surface, Jesus seemed to be repeating Himself—but He wasn't. Jesus used two different words for love when questioning Peter. The first two times Jesus asked Peter if he loved Him, He used the word *agapeo*, which is an intentional, sacrificial love expressed through service. Both times, Peter responded using the word *phileo*, which indicates affection or brotherhood felt for someone with whom you share history. Peter didn't quite get it.[1]

Jesus wanted more from Peter than affection; Jesus wanted Peter to love Him intentionally by serving those who would put their faith in Him after He ascended back into heaven. Once Peter understood, he agreed. After Pentecost (see Acts 2), when the Holy Spirit came to live in Peter as a result of his faith in Jesus, Peter proclaimed the gospel of Jesus with boldness and lived it out with the same gentleness Jesus had shown him.

delight

What evidence can you offer to prove your love for Jesus goes beyond your emotional affection for Him?

Why is it so important for you to show gentleness toward brothers and sisters in Christ who have made mistakes?

display

Make a list of mistakes you have made. Understanding Jesus died on the cross for past, present, and future sin, write the word *forgiven* over each item on your list so that it is crossed out. Let yourself feel the relief of knowing you are forgiven and that God wants to use you to rescue and restore others.

Thank God for forgiving you and giving you a chance to prove your sincere love for Jesus by serving others. Ask God to guide and empower you as you share the gospel of Jesus and restore discouraged sisters in Christ with gentleness.

Poured Out

DAY 27

JESUS' GENTLE CARE

READ 1 PETER 5:6-9.

Humble yourselves, therefore, under the mighty hand of
God, so that he may exalt you at the proper time, casting
all your cares on him, because he cares about you.
—1 Peter 5:6-7

Even the most committed children of God can become consumed with arrogance if they are not careful. Arrogance can happen when we take our focus off of God as the source of our strength and put it on ourselves and our own abilities. God doesn't want us to be arrogant; He wants to work through us. As long as we are focused on ourselves, He can't do that.

What is the antidote to arrogance? Humility. Arrogance leads us to do things that don't reflect Jesus and get in the way of our collective mission. To be good ministers of reconciliation between God and other people, we must humble ourselves, focus on the gospel of Jesus, commit our hearts to rest in His power to save and sustain, and look for opportunities to proclaim, prove, and practice His love by loving others like Jesus did.

When we humble ourselves as Peter instructed, we learn to cast our cares on God. Learning to release our cares to Him and seeing how He handles us with gentleness stirs our hearts to deeper love for Him. As we do this, He lifts us up in His timing and for His glory. He also helps us fight off the attacks of the enemy, who prowls around like a lion looking for someone to devour (v. 8).

delight

How have you seen God's gentle care for you displayed in your life?

How do you strive toward humility in your life?

display

Re-read 1 Peter 5:8-9 and write yourself a letter. In this letter, remind yourself whom you belong to, what your purpose in life is, and what you have to do to fulfill that purpose. Give yourself tips for recognizing and resisting the enemy's attacks. Remind yourself that people who behave badly aren't your enemies— they're victims of the enemy.

> **Thank God for handling the enemy so you don't have to. Ask God to give you compassion for people Satan uses. Commit to staying sober-minded and alert and focusing on the gospel of Jesus.**

DAY 28

JESUS' GENTLE IMITATORS

discover

READ HEBREWS 13:7-8.

Remember your leaders who have spoken God's word to you.
As you carefully observe the outcome of their lives, imitate their
faith. Jesus Christ is the same yesterday, today, and forever.

We must be careful when choosing role models and deciding how much influence to give them. We should listen to people who hold up God's Word, the Bible, as the ultimate authority. We should also only imitate these people if their words and actions prove they believe it.

We all make mistakes. This being true, we must keep a watchful eye on those whom we have chosen to imitate to make sure they do not step off the path God laid out for us and take us with them. If they do step off the path, we must correct them with gentleness and stay the original course.

Christian celebrities on any scale can make people think they know more than others and that they get to change the rules. The Bible says God gives wisdom to anyone who asks and that the Holy Spirit teaches all of God's children. When what someone tells you contradicts what the Holy Spirit says, believe the Holy Spirit—it always matches the Bible.

God does not change, and what He expects does not change. Jesus was consistent in obedience; the earthly examples we follow must strive to do the same.

delight

Why is it so important to keep praying and studying the Bible for yourself even after you think you've found a good role model?

What harm could come from not correcting a child of God whose words, actions, and/or attitudes do not line up with the Bible?

display

Make a list of your role models.

Go back and cross out anyone who does not consider God's Word, the Bible, to be the ultimate authority in their lives. From the remaining list, circle names of those people whose words, actions, and attitudes actually line up with the Bible.

Thank God for people who proclaim the truth according to His Word and live by it. Ask God to give you the opportunity to influence others the same way and to send you brothers and sisters who are brave enough to hold you accountable with gentleness.

Poured Out

JESUS' GENTLE EXAMPLE

discover

READ 1 TIMOTHY 4:12.

Don't let anyone despise your youth, but set an example for the believers in speech, in conduct, in love, in faith, and in purity.

In this letter, the apostle Paul wasn't telling Timothy, his son in the faith, to stick up for himself, but to make sure he didn't do anything to discredit himself as he led the people God had put in his care.

When God accomplishes good things through one of His faithful children, the enemy does his best to undermine that person's influence. He whispers lies and stirs doubts and jealousy—anything to put people at odds with one another. Knowing the enemy could use Timothy's age against him, Paul warned Timothy not to give anyone who might have questions about his age any reason to think he was unqualified to serve.

When challenged, our natural human response is to fight, but Paul suggested a more gentle response. He knew that by setting an example for others in speech, conduct, love, faith, and purity, Timothy would not only prove himself ready to lead, but also shift public focus from himself to God.

True leaders do not allow public opinion, position, title, status, or lack thereof to stand in the way of doing God's will. They simply take care of the opportunities God does give them with grateful hearts and trust Him to make their obedience count as they follow Jesus' example.

delight

How do you usually respond when people question your integrity, intentions, or qualifications to do what God has called you to do? What does this prove?

Why is it important to keep growing spiritually even after God has given you a position of leadership?

display

Consider how setting a better example in speech, conduct, love, faith, and purity could impact the quality and effectiveness of your leadership.

Write a few sentences describing the kind of leader you want to be.

Thank God for not showing favoritism and for giving the same Holy Spirit to everyone who puts their faith in Jesus, regardless of age. Thank God for giving you opportunities to lead people by example. Ask God to increase your influence as you learn to glorify Him in your life.

DAY 30

JESUS' GENTLE REVOLUTION

discover

READ ACTS 17:1-9.

*When they did not find them, they dragged Jason and some
of the brothers before the city officials, shouting, "These men
who have turned the world upside down have come here, too,
and Jason has welcomed them. They are all acting contrary to
Caesar's decrees, saying that there is another king—Jesus."*
—*Acts 17:6-7*

No one comes to the Father unless the Holy Spirit draws them, and
the gospel of Jesus is foolishness to those who do not believe. This
being true, the gospel sometimes stirs conflict—but this conflict
must never become the aim of God's children. Conflict is just a side
effect to be weathered, not a goal to be achieved.

God's children are to be peacemakers, ministers of reconciliation
between God and people. Our calling is to proclaim, prove, and
practice the gospel of Jesus after His own example for God's glory.
If conflict results from our obedience, God will use it, but if we stir
conflict ourselves by doing more than God has called us to do, we
could interfere with His plans.

There is a right way to live poured out—completely devoted
to Jesus—and there is a wrong way—fully devoted to self-
preservation. The gospel of Jesus has the power to do it the right
way. As long as we stay true to this gospel and obedient to our
calling, we will get to be part of it.

delight

How does the potential for conflict usually affect your obedience to God?

What kind of damage can be done by one child of God who uses the gospel of Jesus to stir conflict?

display

Write the words *poured out* on an index card and place it in your Bible, on your bathroom mirror, on the dashboard of your car, or anywhere you'll frequently see it. Remember that God has called you to a revolution to live poured out, learning to lead humbly and gently, just like Jesus.

Thank God for sending Jesus to rescue the world from sin. Thank God for allowing you to participate in His mission by proclaiming, proving, and practicing the gospel. Ask God to help you turn the world upside down like Jesus' disciples did, through faithful obedience, servant leadership, and gentle love.

A GENTLE HEART

When people hear the word *gentleness,* they often think of women. The Bible does say that a woman's beauty should flow outwardly from her "gentle and quiet spirit" (1 Pet. 3:5). Although women were called to be gentle then (as we are now), the culture in Jesus' day, even among the Jews, didn't exactly extend gentleness toward women. They were restricted in worship, both in public and at home. Conversations with women were limited, even between husband and wife. A good woman was to listen, not speak, and some even believed she shouldn't be allowed to touch the Scriptures because she might "defile them."[2]

But as you grow to expect from Jesus through reading the Gospels, He was different. In no way did He match the image the Jews had painted of their Messiah. This extended into His treatment of women. In fact, some of Jesus' closest followers were women. While today's women are generally treated with greater respect than those in Jesus' day, every culture still has some kind of "shape" or type of woman that is considered ideal—one that often devalues or discriminates against women in some way.

If we follow Jesus' way of doing things today, we will look different from the rest of the world. But that's the life we're called to: We are to be holy and set apart, even as we live in and love the world around us. In regard to our identity as daughters of God and the other girls around us, we are called to extend the same gentle compassion and love that Jesus did. But sometimes even girls struggle to view themselves with a gentle heart, let alone treat other girls with gentleness. So, let's take a look at some of Jesus' interactions with women in the Bible and see what each one teaches us about being gentle with ourselves and others.

Mary, the mother of Jesus. Read Luke 2:48; 8:19-20; John 2:1-12 and 19:26-27. Jesus' first recorded miracle was at the request of His mother at a wedding in Cana, and one of His last commands on the cross was about His mother, too. Even when Mary didn't understand what Jesus was doing or why He did things a certain way, He was respectful and gentle. He also tenderly cared for her in making sure she would be provided for after His death, resurrection, and ascension to the Father.

What does His gentleness in this situation teach you about the gentleness He also extends to you when you don't understand His actions?

How does it teach you to respond in gentleness to girls who might not understand your faith?

The Samaritan Woman. Read John 4:6-30. Jesus went through a place most Jews avoided (Samaria) to speak with a woman most people avoided. Jesus opened their conversation with a seemingly simple question, but in His asking, He reached out to a woman who may have felt unreachable and unworthy of being seen. This woman's shame was the theme song of her life. His question led to talking about more than just water from the well where they were sitting; it led to Him introducing her to the living water—"the gift of the Holy Spirit, who grants eternal life to those in whom He dwells"[3]—that only He could provide. Jesus gently and boldly confronted her sin, but He also lovingly pointed her to the solution.

How has He done the same for you?

What does His gentleness as He stepped into this woman's story teach you about the way you should view your own story? About how you should step into others' stories?

The Woman Caught in Adultery. Read John 8:3-11. While the blame lay on both the man and the woman caught in this situation, the Jewish leaders only brought the woman before Jesus, pointing out that the Old Testament Law demanded she be stoned. They brought her shame to the forefront, ignoring their own. But Jesus pointed them back to the truth that they, too, were sinners. When no one stood left to condemn the woman, Jesus spoke these gentle words to her: "Neither do I condemn you...Go, and from now on do not sin anymore" (v. 11). They had focused on her sin; He led her to forgiveness from it.

How do you see Jesus' gentleness most clearly displayed in this interaction?

What do His words to the Pharisees and the woman teach you about being gentle with others' shame while not ignoring their sin?

What does this story teach you about the way Jesus extends forgiveness to you, even when you feel weighed down by shame?

Mary and Martha. Read Matthew 26:6-13; Mark 14:3-9; Luke 10:38-42; John 11:1-46. Scripture says Jesus loved their family. We see this in every interaction He had with them—even after Lazarus' death. Jesus met Mary and Martha where they were. He met Martha in her busyness and Mary in her desire to learn. He met them both in their grief and in their questions. He met them in their moments of faith, too. He also defended Mary when the disciples scolded her for anointing Him with expensive perfume, pointing out that she did "a noble thing" (Matt. 26:10).

What are the similarities and differences of the way Jesus interacted with Mary and with Martha? How do both reveal His gentleness?

How does Jesus' unique gentleness toward both women teach us to treat people with gentleness for who they are instead of frustration for who they aren't?

Mary Magdalene. Read Mark 15:40,47–16:1-11; John 20:11-18. Mary began following Jesus after He healed her by casting seven (yes, seven) demons out of her (see Mark 16:11.) Although women were typically restricted from being part of a ministry, Mary supported Jesus' ministry "from [her] possessions" (Luke 8:3). She was present at His crucifixion, followed to see where He was buried, went to prepare His body for burial with the other women, and was the first person Jesus appeared to after His resurrection. When Jesus wasn't in the tomb, Mary was distraught. Jesus saw her tears, and the moment He said her name, she recognized Him. She was the one He sent to carry the good news of His resurrection to the disciples.

How do you see Jesus' gentleness displayed in the way He both healed and appeared to Mary after His resurrection?

What does Jesus' tenderness toward Mary's tears show you about His tenderness toward yours?

How does this teach you to respond to other girls' pain with gentleness, too?

Honestly, we could comb through the pages of the New Testament and find countless stories of Jesus healing women no one else would go near, of Him honoring their faith, and of Him healing daughters for mourning fathers and sons for mourning mothers. He treated women with respect, dignity, and gentleness as invited them to be healed and to follow Him. Many answered His call. Will you?

NOTES

Use this space to tuck away the truths that stand out to you from Jesus' interactions with women.

Poured Out

SOURCES

1. "Why did Jesus ask Peter 'Do you love me?' three times?" https://www.gotquestions.org/Jesus-Peter-do-you-love-me.html

2. Evelyn Stagg and Frank Stagg, "Jesus and Women," Christian History | Learn the History of Christianity & the Church (Christian History, January 1, 1988), https://www.christianitytoday.com/history/issues/issue-17/jesus-and-women.html.

3. Ed Stetzer, "Living Water That Satisfies Completely," The Exchange | A Blog by Ed Stetzer (Christianity Today, June 26, 2020), https://www.christianitytoday.com/edstetzer/2020/june/living-water-that-satisfies-completely.html.